Presents
United We Quilt
& Anchor Project

American Quilter's Society

P. O. Box 3290 • Paducah, KY 42002-3290

www.AQSquilt.com

Located in Paducah, Kentucky, the American Quilter's Society (AQS) is dedicated to promoting the accomplishments of today's quilters. Through its publications and events, AQS strives to honor today's quiltmakers and their work and to inspire future creativity and innovation in quiltmaking.

BOOK EDITOR: HELEN SQUIRE
GRAPHIC DESIGN: MICHAEL BUCKINGHAM
COVER DESIGN: MICHAEL BUCKINGHAM
PHOTOGRAPHY: CHARLES R. LYNCH
UNITED WE QUILT EDITOR: BARBARA SMITH
ANCHOR PROJECT EDITOR: MARJORIE RUSSELL

Library of Congress Cataloging-in-Publication Data

AQS Presents United We Quilt & Anchor Project / by the American Quilter's Society
    p. cm.
    ISBN 1-57432-806-9
1. Quilts--United States--History--20th century--Themes, motives. 2. September 11 Terrorist Attacks, 2001--Art and the terrorist attacks. I. American Quilter's Society. II. United We Quilt (Project : U.S.)
NK9112 .A69 2002
746.46'0973--dc21

        2002005000

Additional copies of this book may be ordered from the American Quilter's Society, PO Box 3290, Paducah, KY 42002-3290, or online at www.AQSquilt.com.

CONTENTS

AQS authors create a special tribute

United We Quilt ★★★

Quilters share their sympathy & grief

Anchor Project ★★★

INTRODUCTION

The **UNITED WE QUILT** exhibit grew out of the events of September 11, 2001. In adversity, quilters quite naturally turn to needle and thread, and quilting can bring great comfort, not only to those who make the quilts, but to those who view them as well.

detail – *Liberty*, pg. 9

"...to create a quilt in the spirit of hope and healing."

The **AMERICAN QUILTER'S SOCIETY** invited authors from its first 16 years of publishing books on patchwork, appliqué, and quilting to create a quilt in the spirit of hope and healing for nationwide exhibition.

THE EXHIBIT previewed at the AQS shows in Paducah, Kentucky, and Nashville, Tennessee. Then it was divided into two parts to be shown at other venues, from museums and quilt conventions to local quilt guilds. Both parts of the exhibit are balanced for artistic appeal and can be displayed separately or together.

detail – *The American Spirit Lives On*, pg. 37

The fees for hosting the traveling exhibition vary, based on venue size (shipping and insurance additional). All profits will be given by the American Quilter's Society to the *New York Police and Fire Widow's and Children's Benefit Fund*, *NOVA (National Organization for Victim Assistance)*, and the *American Rescue Dog Association*.

detail – *The Patriot Dream*, pg. 24

AQS Presents United We Quilt & Anchor Project

FEATURED are a representation of stencilling, appliqué, pieced, and quilted surfaces, all within certain size guidelines. Marvel at the variety of techniques used. As you turn the pages and read the text, notice how often hand and machine sewing was combined. View contemporary designs as well as meaningful traditional patterns.

detail – *God Bless America*, pg. 14

detail – *In God We Trust*, pg. 10

The **SYMBOLS OF AMERICA**, our flag and the eagle, were the most frequent choices of our authors. Famous, historic words were embroidered, appliquéd, penned, or quilted, to remind us of our heritage. New phrases have been added: "Let's Roll," the President's message, and the names of those fallen from the tragic events of "The Eleventh."

AQS proudly acknowledges the extraordinary efforts of Barbara Smith, executive book editor, for coordinating *United We Quilt* and arranging its exhibition schedule. We want to thank all participating **AUTHORS**, and apologize that time and space prohibited showcasing every quilt.

detail – *Liberty Enlightens*, pg. 35

After all that has just passed – all the lives taken, and all the possibilities and hopes that died with them – it is natural to wonder if America's future is one of fear. Some speak of an age of terror. I know there are struggles ahead, and dangers to face. But this country will define our times, not be defined by them. As long as the United States of America is determined and strong, this will not be an age of terror; this will be an age of liberty, here and across the world.

Great harm has been done to us. We have suffered great loss. And in our grief and anger we have found our mission and our moment. Freedom and fear are at war. The advance of human freedom – the great achievement of our time, and the great hope of every time – now depends on us. Our nation – this generation – will lift a dark threat of violence from our people and our future. We will rally the world to this cause by our efforts, by our courage. We will not tire, we will not falter, and we will not fail.

President George W. Bush
September 20, 2001

detail – *The Age of Liberty*, pg. 38

QUILTMAKERS use cloth, color, ink, and thread to express their feelings – as viewers, we can all relate. Expect to see fabric combinations from somber to vibrant, all done with a message... and a prayer for hope and healing.

AQS Presents United We Quilt & Anchor Project

5

United We Stand

by Sue Nickels • machine pieced, appliquéd, and quilted. 42" x 42"

Author of
Machine Appliqué:
A Sampler of Techniques

There was an immediate patriotic response to the attacks against our country. Flags could be seen on houses, businesses, and cars. Even road signs had our flag displayed with the simple statement, "United we stand."

Let's Roll

by Lois Embree Arnold

reverse hand appliquéd, machine pieced and quilted. 50" x 41"

On September 11, lives were lost, heroes were born, faith was re-examined, and patriotism was renewed. No American was unaffected, and one American, Todd Beamer, immortalized the words, "Let's Roll!"

Author of
Pine Tree Quilts:
Perfect Patchwork Piecing

Day of Infamy
by Susan McKelvey
hand pieced, appliquéd, quilted, and pen & ink. 53" x 53"

Author of
Fancy Feathered Friends for Quilters

September 11 was a nation-shaping event that will not be forgotten. I designed my tribute to be uplifting, encompassing significant images from both our national and quilt heritages.

Liberty
by Suzanne Marshall

machine pieced, and hand appliquéd, embroidered, and quilted. 39½" x 45½"

Throughout our history, there have been expressions of patriotism in quiltmaking prompted by pride or tragedy. When making "Liberty," I was especially inspired by an eagle on an appliqué quilt made in 1807.

Author of
Take Away Appliqué

In God We Trust
by Marie Sturmer

stenciled whole cloth, cotton embroidery, and hand quilted. 36" x 47"

Author of
Stencil Quilts for Chirstmas

To trust in God gives confidence in an all-loving and caring power that sustains man in every adverse situation. Francis Scott Key wrote of this in the "Star-Spangled Banner." This trust was expressed once again in 1864 when the words "In God We Trust" appeared on U.S. coins.

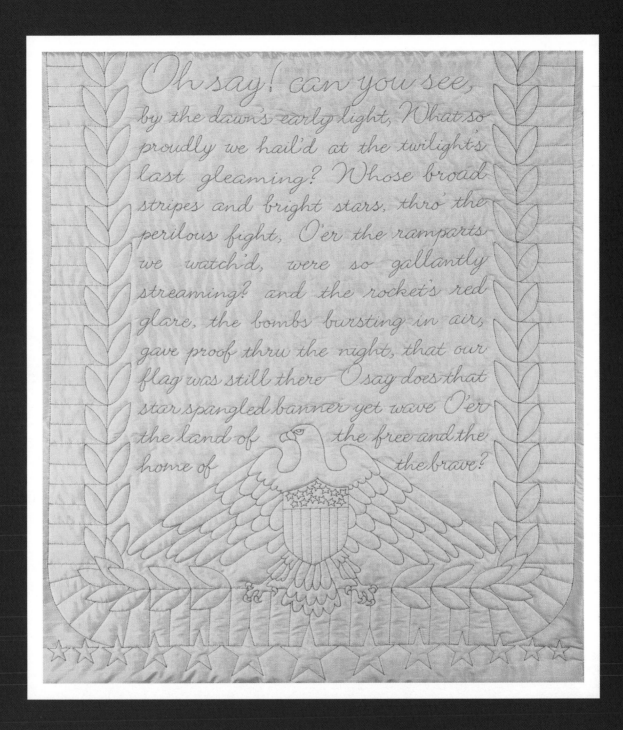

Oh Say! Can You See?

by Helen Squire • hand quilted on 100% Dupioni silk. 40" x 45½"

I saw a photograph once of a quilt on which the words of "The Star-Spangled Banner" were quilted. The memory of that simple, eloquent quilt became my inspiration to take Francis Scott Key's patriotic words and quilt them into cloth for all to see and remember.

Quilting Designs
by Helen Squire, *Helen's Copy & Use Quilting Patterns*, and by Michael Buckingham, *Presidential Redwork*.

Patriotic Quilt
by Gwen Marston

machine pieced, hand and machine appliquéd, and hand quilted. 49" x 49"

Author of
Fabric Picture Books, Liberated Quiltmaking, Quilting with Style, American Beauty Rose and Tulip & Sets and Borders

When the words patriotic and quilts appear in the same sentence, my mind turns immediately to the Pennsylvania German eagle quilts from the mid-1880s. This quilt is a reminder of the traumatic events of September 11.

Let Freedom Ring
by Bea Oglesby

hand and machine appliquéd, and hand quilted. 41" x 41"

The Preamble to the Constitution begins with the words, "We the people." With the First Amendment, our freedoms of religion, speech, press, and assembly are guaranteed. Let Freedom Ring.

Author of

Wildflower Album: Appliqué & Embroidery Patterns

God Bless America
by Anita Shackelford
machine pieced, hand and machine appliquéd and quilted. 40" x 41"

Author of
Infinite Feathers,
Coxcomb Variations,
Appliqué with Folded Cutwork,
and Surface Textures

Out of chaos came rediscovery of human kindness, strength of spirit, love of country, and heroes who were always there. Let us be grateful to live in a country where we can pray, sing, say, and shout "God Bless America!"

Triumph
by Gail Searl
machine pieced, hand and machine quilted. 45½" x 45½"

Ground level discloses destruction, a landscape of ashes and flame, until one twisted girder emerges, revealed as a cross of Christ. Now, united we stand, safe in the shelter of our Lord, embraced by freedom, triumphant!

Author of
*Sew Many Stars:
Technique & Patterns*

On Eagles' Wings
by Barbara W. Barber
machine pieced, embroidered, and quilted. 45" x 45"

Author of
Broderie Perse:
AQS Love to Quilt Series

Our homeland, which is symbolized in this quilt by Log Cabin blocks, was attacked. Out of the flames and ashes, we rise united and strengthened. "He renews our strength like the eagles," Psalms 103:5.

Nonetheless, We Shall Prevail
by Betty Alderman

fusible-web appliquéd, machine pieced and quilted. 47½" x 45"

Designed two months before September 11, my quilt seemed eerily prophetic in the aftermath of that day. I added the words when I heard my pastor speak of "the faithfulness of God, nonetheless."

Author of
Favorite Redwork Designs

Our Heroes of 9-11 and Beyond
by **Donna French Collins**
hand appliquéd and quilted on hand-dyed fabrics. 48" x 46½"

Author of
Spike & Zola: Patterns Designed for Laughter... and Appliqué, Painting, or Stenciling

We will never forget the many people who perished on September 11. The police and firefighters risk their lives every day. They stand as tall as the Twin Towers stood.

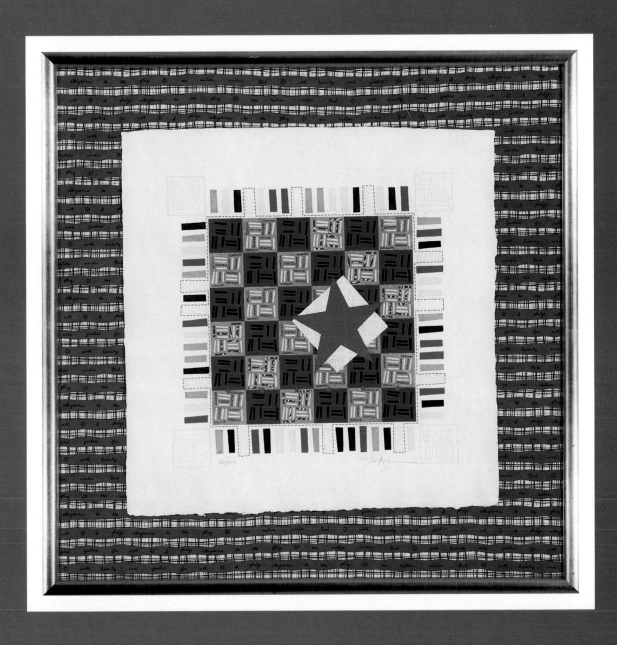

Allegiance
by Rod Buffington
watercolor collage on handmade paper, 100% cotton fabric. 30" x 30"

A restless feeling developed as I stood alone with tears of disbelief, watching anxious individuals staggering to cope with tragedy. The allegiance to the flag gives each of us an opportunity to stand united.

Author & curator of
*Double Vision:
Companions & Choices*

Together
by Joan Waldman
machine appliquéd, pieced, and quilted. 41" x 41"

Author of
Pick-A-Pattern Appliqué & Variations and Flower Patterns to Appliqué, Paint & Embroider

"Together" represents all who band together to quilt during times of stress. The red, white, and blue broken circles represent the fracturing of our peace on September 11.

20

AQS Presents United We Quilt & Anchor Project

A Memorial Tribute – September 11, 2001

by Faye Labanaris

hand appliquéd and quilted. 43" x 43"

I originally created this design to commemorate peace after the 1991 Gulf War. After September 11, however, the design was re-stitched to memorialize the precious lives lost.

Author of
Garden View Appliqué,
Quilts with a View, and
Blossoms by the Sea

Betsy's Flag
by Pennie Horras
machine pieced and appliquéd, hand and machine quilted. 34½" x 42½"

Author of
*Sewing in Circles:
Easy Machine Appliqué
Quilts*

Stars and stripes have become part of the greatest symbols of freedom around the world. As hearts were breaking on September 11 and we prayed for hope and healing, our flag was there, symbolizing the unity and strength of our nation.

Love Conquers All

by Jeanie Sexton • Free-motion-machine embroidered with metallic super-twist thread, machine pieced, appliquéd, and quilted. 48" x 41½"

The flag is outline quilted with jagged lines, then softly stipple quilted to the edge, symbolizing tattered lives that are softened with love. Faith in God's love gave me the strength to hope as my son flew south from Chicago. "I'm safe in Atlanta, Mom, and I love you."

Author of
Silk Ribbons by Machine

That Sees Beyond the Years

O Beautiful for Patriot Dream

Thine Alabaster Cities Gleam

Undimmed by Human Tears

The Patriot Dream
by DeLoa Dawn Jones
machine embroidered, pieced, appliquéd and quilted; heat-set crayon. 43½" x 48"

Author of
Scraps Organized to Perfection

The Patriot Dream stirs within our hearts. The teardrop quilting, combined with a smoky backing, symbolizes our mourning of the attack, but the Twin Towers will remain in our memories.

United We Stand
by Rita Denenberg
machine appliquéd. 46" x 36"

The woman featured in this quilt is tearful, yet defiant. She represents my feelings. With my tears lessened, I am still sad, but defiant as ever that we stand strong as a nation.

Author of
*Rhyme-Time Blocks:
Appliqué & Embroidery
Patterns*

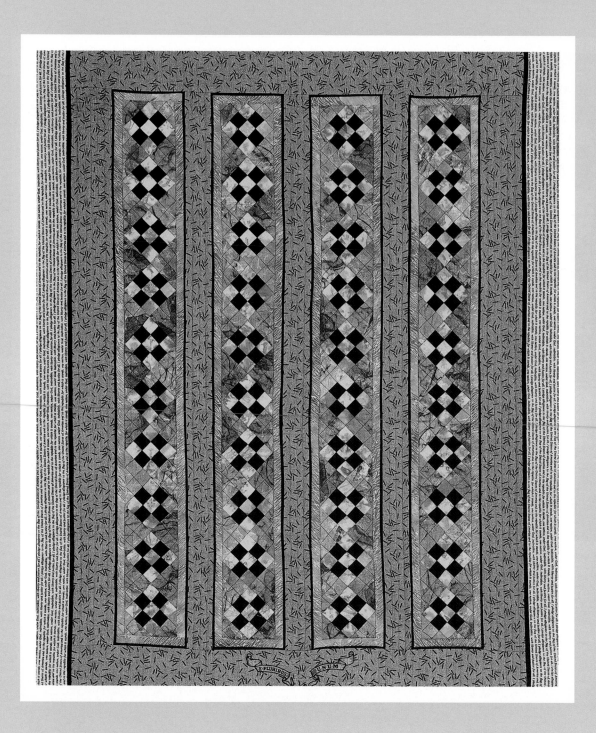

United We Grieve
by **Nancy S. Breland**
machine pieced and quilted. 40" x 47½"

Author of
Tricks with Chintz:
Using Large Prints to Add
New Magic to Traditional
Quilt Blocks

September 11 left America with images of destruction. Through our shared grief, we have strengthened our dedication to "one nation, under God, indivisible, with liberty, and justice for all."

26

Dawns a New Day
by Laura Lee Fritz
machine quilted on four layers of wool-rayon felt. 49" x 47"

The wool felt provided the perfect medium for the spontaneous eruption of spirit. It communicates the boldness of change and the softness of heart. This quilt was made to remind us that we always have a new dawn coming.

Author of
The Art of Hand Appliqué

To Defend Forever the Flames of Freedom
by Scarlett Rose
hand appliquéd Celtic knotwork, machine pieced and quilted. 40" x 58"

Author of
Baskets: Celtic Style and
Celtic Style Appliqué

Whether represented by the torch of the Statue of Liberty or the candlelight vigils after September 11, the symbols of the flame and the shield remind all that we must never waver in our dedication to the cause of freedom.

Bethlehem Silks

by Dianne S. Hire

machine appliquéd, pieced, and quilted. 48½" x 50"

The diverse colors, which were chosen to represent the uniqueness of humanity, brought to mind the words of a simple children's song: "Red and yellow, black and white, we are precious in His sight. Jesus loves the little children of the world."

Co-editor of
Oxymorons:
Absurdly Logical Quilts

Phoenix Rose
by Letty Martin
machine pieced and appliquéd. 39½" x 45½"

Author of
Straight Stitch Machine Appliqué: History, Patterns & Instructions for This Easy Technique

As the Phoenix rose to life from the ashes, so will America rebuild. The rose, our national flower, symbolizes the hope and determination of the people.

Recycled Hearts
by Faye Anderson
hand appliquéd, machine pieced and quilted. 44" x 44"

Our hearts and lives have been broken, but they are being mended in ways we could not have foreseen. Perhaps tolerance and appreciation of diversity are the greatest lessons we could learn.

Author of
Appliqué Designs: My Mother Taught Me to Sew

Stars & Stripes
by Marianne Fons & Liz Porter
machine pieced, appliquéd, and quilted. 44" x 50"

Co-authors of
Classic Basket Quilts

Stars and stripes, the American eagle holding emblems of war and peace, a schoolhouse where one learns the ABCs — these symbols of America are inextricably woven into the history of American quilting.

USA Forever
by Marianne Fons & Liz Porter
machine pieced, appliquéd, and quilted. 51" x 42"

Quilters find comfort through the act of quilting. Thankfully, our minds are free to wander while we sew. As Americans, we are free to express our thoughts by speaking, writing, voting, and the images we portray in our quilts.

Co-authors of
Classic Basket Quilts

What So Proudly We Hailed
by Linda Carlson
hand appliquéd, machine pieced and quilted. 43" x 43"

Author of
Roots, Feathers, and Blooms
and *Four Blocks Continued*

This block is infused with heart-wrenching symbolism. The star tips were cut off to represent the attack, then appliquéd back in place to represent the heroic efforts of the rescue teams and volunteers.

Liberty Enlightens
by Joyce B. Peaden

hand and machine pieced, hand appliquéd, embroidered, and quilted. 42" x 50"

This quilt consists of traditional blocks composed of world-wide symbols of liberty, creativity, and prudence, including the Crown and Cross for England and law, wheat for benevolence, and white oak for bravery.

Author of
Irish Chain Quilts:
A Workbook of Irish Chains
and Related Patterns

Our Light Shines On
by Sharon Stroud
hand appliquéd and quilted. 40" x 40"

Author of
Dresden Plates: AQS Love to Quilt Series

Inspired by a photograph from the 1875 Centennial celebration, this quilt represents our hope for the future, illuminated by the torch of the Statue of Liberty.

The American Spirit Lives On
by Carol Shoaf
hand appliquéd and machine quilted. 40" x 46"

Stan Lee said September 11 was "A day Liberty lost her heart and found the strength within her soul." In this quilt, the American spirit surrounds the victims with the best of our American ideals.

Co-author of
Marbling Fabrics for Quilts: A Guide for Learning and Teaching

The Age of Liberty
by Judy Mercer Tescher
original fabric, machine pieced and quilted. 43½" x 48½"

Author of
Dyeing and Overdyeing Cotton Fabrics

How can humans harbor hate so great that it demands killing thousands of people? That kind of hate is not in me nor is it in my friends and family, perhaps because we live in a land of liberty.

Quilters throughout history have responded to crisis by making quilts. The **ANCHOR PROJECT** asked for 9-inch blocks in America's favorite colors: red, white, and blue. Quilts made from the blocks were destined for auction to raise funds for post-September 11 needs. Signed individual blocks express symbolic messages – our anchors in the face of crisis and terrorism. Groups volunteering to assemble the blocks had the honor of naming the quilts. Assemblers and quilters were identified on the permanent back labels. We appreciate the giving spirit – evidenced in time, materials, and design – that made this project possible, and are very grateful for everyone's support.

Marjorie Russell, executive editor of *American Quilter* magazine, is the originator and coordinator of the Anchor Project. Special thanks also go to Lisa Clark, Lynda Smith, and Tom Sullivan, AQS graphic designers, who are responsible for the exceptional level of professionalism achieved. This book is dedicated to Meredith Schroeder, founder and president of the **AMERICAN QUILTER'S SOCIETY**. Her leadership, faith, and encouragement shine through every AQS project.

Proceeds from the online auction of the finished quilts will be donated to the *New York Police and Fire Widow's and Children's Benefit Fund, National Organization for Victim Assistance (NOVA)*, and *American Rescue Dog Association*.

Anchor Project
QUILTS

Anchor project AQS

INTRODUCTION

An outpouring of sympathy and grief by quilters from across America and the world in memory of the events of September 11, 2001

The total number of blocks received closely paralleled the number of fatalities in New York, Washington, DC, and Pennsylvania.

• • • TIMELINE • • •

INITIATED the Anchor Project with e-mail and *American Quilter* magazine announcements. Within 12 weeks received blocks from all 50 states and 17 countries.

COORDINATED groups of blocks and sent them to volunteers who, in 6 weeks, assembled them together.

MAILED tops to quilters who had only 4 weeks to machine or hand quilt, bind, and return finished quilts.

Book preparation accomplished in 3 weeks, including quilt photography, documentation, and exhibition plans. At press time, completed quilts were still arriving. This is only a small sampling of the total quilts to be **AUCTIONED**.

Thoughts...

"I have made this quilt block in honor of my son, Commander Lowell David Crow, United States Navy and in memory of his shipmates who died at the Pentagon."
Sondra K. Crow, Rolla, MO

"My heart, thoughts, and prayers go out to all the victims, their families, relatives, and friends – of the unspeakable act of terrorism that was committed."
Judie Medjanyk, Spooner, WI

"The world is a very different place since 11 September 2001. Together we can comfort and support each other through difficult times. My thoughts are with you all in the USA."
Margaret Davidson, Wolverhampton, England

"Our American heart has been tragically wounded and torn to pieces. Today, under God, we mend and heal and are united even stronger."
Emmy Schmidt, Evansville, IN

"Justice will prevail. I thought Courthouse Steps would be an an appropriate pattern to symbolize that our American Spirit will win out. GOD BLESS AMERICA."
Mrs. Olive Dmochowski, Stamford, CT

"Thank you for offering me a way to respond to tragedy with warmth and beauty in the form of an American quilt."
Katie Winchell, Asheville, NC

"As I cut and sewed each block, my husband and I prayed for the victims, the families, and our country. From evil, God can turn a situation into one for good and His glory. We have seen examples of this in the heroism and the loving compassion which has occurred all over the country."
Daisy & Robert Kemper, Maden, NC

"May you find peace, comfort, and love in your life. May God hold us all in his hands."
Becky Yurchiak, Barkerton, OK

"There are no words to adequately express the depth of feelings we have for all the victims and families – hopefully this small token of love will somehow bring a measure of comfort."
Pam Weyenberg, Kingsbury, CA

"My feelings of sadness and grief have been overtaken with intense pride in the unity that the people of our country have found. UNITED WE STAND! And God Bless America!"
Richelle Shetina, Ponchatoula, LA

"NEW YORK BEAUTY SHOWS HER COLORS symbolizes for me that each of us can make a difference by acts of loving kindness."
Alberta M. Richmond, Waban, MA

"Because my husband and I are active EMT/Firefighters, we very much appreciated this project and say THANK YOU to all the quilters who participated."
Jerry & Louise Gramley, Reedsville, PA

"Our country stands united as it did when the stitches of hope and faith gave birth to our first flag. Let the common threads of freedom and democracy comfort us through these times."
L. Pomes, Frankfort, IL

"We, the people of the United States of America, will never let the terrorists win! With our love of God, our country, and each other, we will triumph."
Beverly Deutsch Moore, Yorkville, IL

"I am an Australian living in Hong Kong and I felt that I would like to participate in making some blocks for the appeal to benefit the families of the September 11, 2001, attack. My heart has been heavy since that awful day... may your grief be short but the memories of those people last forever."
Florence Shannon, Hong Kong, China

"Thank you, AQS, for this patriotic Anchor Project. I hope funds raised can help ease the pain of victims of the World Trade Center tragedy. Our prayers are with the families of the fallen heroes, for their selfless acts of heroism."
Kate Crites, Upper Glade, WV

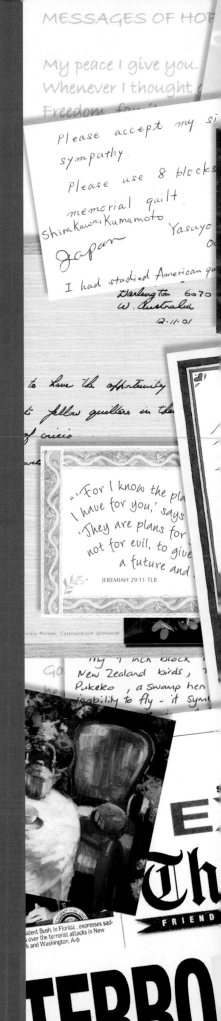

"I have chosen a schoolhouse block because I believe it is only through education and humanitarian aid that we can achieve lasting peace and understanding."

Mary Brown, State College, PA

"My block reminds me of a happy childhood July 4th holiday because of the pinwheel. Let us hope and pray we can once again begin to feel safe, secure, and happy in friendship and love as small children do."

Elizabeth Janowitz, Pinecrest, FL

"Our four-year-old grandson said: 'I don't have to pray for the victims – they're in heaven. I pray for their families because they're sad.' Amen."

Louise DuBrule, TX

"It saddens me to think that the tragic events of September 11 had to make us aware of the great country we live in and the privileges we enjoy on a daily basis. We must continue to have patience and compassion for our fellow countrymen."

Paula Leonhard, South Bend, IN

"May each 'star' represent the light of freedom and a hope that one day, all peoples of our world will share and enjoy freedom also."

Jane Brown, Sterling, VA

"September 11 will be permanently etched in all of our minds. May the finished quilts be a positive reminder of our strength, our hopes, and our prayers."

Patricia A. Livengood, Salem, OR

"This block was made in memory of Eric 'Rick' Thorpe who worked on the 89th floor of Tower Two for Keefe, Bruyette & Woods, Inc."

Sandra Carlson, Wilbeaham, MA

"Ten years ago, I became an American citizen, I celebrated with a great patriotic quilt. I kept my fabrics and used some in this candlelight block to tell the world America will keep the light through darkness.

Marie F. Concher, Mamaroneck, NY

"We donate these quilt blocks with the realization that we were fortunate to be born in the United States of America. Tears were shed for the loss of lives … and also for the thought that freedom might be lost forever. We must and will fight for the freedom that we have in the United States of America."

Gladys Keddie, Dunnellon, FL

"These two little blocks are such a small effort on behalf of those who need an anchor in our troubled times. My love travels with them."

Jeannne Williams, Spokane, WA

"A simple Nine-Patch, in remembrance of the day that changed our lives forever. This block is stitched with love and prayers for our nation."

Alma Weilmuenster, Ballwin, MO

"Though we are far apart, our hands joined for love, peace, and friendship will overcome these hard times."

Canan Yalcin, Cankaya-Ankara,Turkey

"God Bless America, all the armed forces, and those leaders of our great country, especially President Bush. Pray for peace, and God's guidance."

Maryann Reese, Twin Falls, ID

"We've made these blocks with the hope that there will be a time when people of different nations, different religions, and from different countries will live in peace, will love each other and respect each other."

Luda Yanchemko, Kazakhstan

"With each stitch we will mend the tear. Our fabric will be even stronger in the end."

Jean Balliro, Saugus, MS

We the People ...
120" x 110"

Embroidered portraits of President George W. Bush and First Lady Laura Bush, and all 42 former United States presidents, are joined with symbolic Americana patterns for a total of **81** blocks. Appliquéd peace roses and a patriotic framework of yellow stars and red and blue stripes surround the couple and the "We the People ..." title.

New Jersey Herald • Newton, New Jersey • January 27, 2002
SUSSEX COUNTY'S DAILY NEWSPAPER

Lifestyle

E1

Presidential assignment

"Part of what makes quilters so special is their willingness to be involved."
Marjorie Russell, Anchor Project coordinator, American Quilter's Society

Photos by Teresa Crerand

PATRIOTIC PROJECT — From left, Milford Valley Quilters Guild members Emmie Lyle, Helen Umstead, ...rol Hill, Barbara Demczak and Mary Murray begin work on a patriotic quilt that will be donated to ...esident and Mrs. Bush. The quilt contains 37 blocks submitted by quilters in the U.S. and abroad as part ...post-Sept. 11 project of the American Quilter's Society. Included are an eagle design (top left) made by ...and, at right, an American flag design by Marge Macchia of Teaneck.

...SA CRERAND
...he New Jersey Herald

...of area quilters has received
...ential task to complete.
...ting their talents to work
...is destined for delivery to
...ge W. Bush and first lady
...onal project the

groups — from schoolchildren who made them as a special project to individual quilters, various quilting groups and some of the 60,000 AQS members.
"Quilters like to quilt and that is how they respond to crisis," explained Russell. "So we thought we would give them an opportunity with our project to be able to submit something that would ...become part

by Fran Perry of Shepshed, England while Moira Watson of Tillicoultry, Scotland, for-warded a patriotic sailboat.
Blocks were received with short quotes or messages of encouragement...

AQS Presents United We Quilt & Anchor Project

Made by a Pennsylvania quilt guild, this quilt represents quiltmakers around the world who were involved in the Anchor Project. The quilt will be presented to the White House in affirmation of the Preamble to the Constitution and the Anchor Project.

Memorial Quilt 71" x 71"

Four stars, plus eight flag patches, plus four hearts
equal **16** blocks made with love. Delectable
Mountains and Flying Geese piecing frames the
uniquely set blocks. Assembled and machine quilted
in California.

Stars and Stripes Forever *57" x 76½"*

Narrow strips form vertical rows between the **40** individual blocks. The same navy fabric is used to border and bind the edges of the quilt. Assembled and machine quilted in Montana.

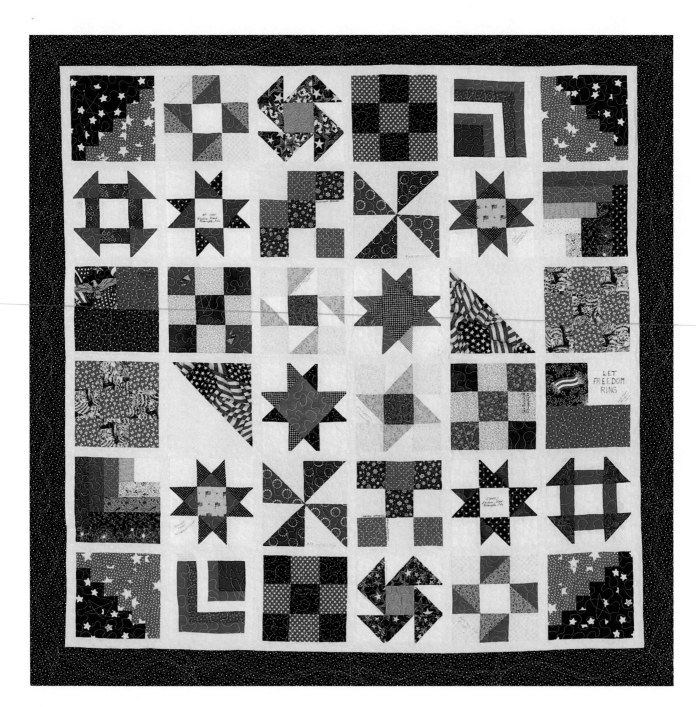

Come Together 65½" x 65½"

The ecru-colored sashing causes the **36** traditional blocks to radiate and permits joining any under-sized blocks. The star motif is most prevalent in the choice of fabric and quilting design. Assembled and machine quilted in Ohio.

Threads of Freedom 56" x 75"

A handsome presentation of narrow sashing with twenty-four mini-stars showcases a variety of **35** blocks. Star blocks are interspersed with channel quilting in the wide borders. Machine pieced and quilted in Maryland.

Let Freedom Ring 65" x 76½"

A thick and thin red, white, and blue triple border surrounds the **30** inner blocks, each set with an intersection square. Free-motion quilting is combined with straight lines. Assembled and quilted in Montana.

Rockets Red Glare 38" x 38"

Set on-point, these **12** pieced star blocks blend together beautifully between the red triangles. Paper-pieced stars and precision-points create a variety of designs. Assembled and machine stipple quilted in South Carolina.

We Are One Country First 40" x 60½"

Freedom, family, faith, and friendship are all represented in the **15** traditional blocks joined with sashing strips and flag-printed borders. Made, assembled, and machine quilted in Alabama.

If Tomorrow Never Comes 54" x 68"

A medallion of four string-pieced center blocks are combined with **20** basic blocks. Finished with window-pane sashing and wide borders. Assembled in Montana and machine quilted in New York.

The Flags of Liberty Still Soar Like an Eagle 60" x 72"

The focal point of this quilt is an eagle and shield in the center of a star medallion. This is surrounded by **21** flag blocks of unique patterns. Designed, pieced, assembled, and quilted in New Mexico.

Patriotic Partners 70" x 70"

Four of the **25** blocks provide extra dimension with their diagonal stripes. The bordered blocks, in two tones of blue, are framed by a red inner border. Assembled and quilted in North Carolina.

Healing Hearts 80" x 80"

These **25** hearts from across America and the world are proudly displayed with patriotic bands of stars and stripes. The theme continues in the corner blocks with hearts and stars combined. Assembled and quilted in Michigan.

Threads of Hope 82½" x 100"

An interesting set of framed and squared-off blocks, all set on-point, is as dynamic as the firework-print border. The elaborate, continuous quilting design adds movement and pizazz to the **32** original blocks. Assembled and quilted in Minnesota.

Red, White & Blue Inspiration   57½" x 78"

All **35** blocks represent bright hopes, loving hearts, and French heritage. Each is set in a color-contrast, double-sashed border. A group quilt, made and hand quilted in New Jersey.

Sawtooth Stars 86" x 86"

The dark navy triangles and bright red squares produce a secondary design to showcase the **16** star blocks. The blocks are set on-point and alternate with a cosmic print fabric. Assembled and machine quilted in Kentucky.

Liberty, Peace, Tears & Hope for Freedom 64½" x 85"

The wide quilted borders handsomely combine **35** popular blocks. The degree of difficulty varies from a New York Beauty design to a basic Nine-Patch. Assembled and machine quilted in Iowa.

Love and Hope – The Fabrics of Our World 80" x 91"

Featuring **42** blocks, this is an excellent example of a sampler quilt. Four mitered borders surround the 6 x 7 block setting. Machine quilting enhances every block. Assembled and quilted in Minnesota.

Patriotic Interpretation *42½" x 52½"*

Stars abound from the New York skyline fabric to the
appliquéd and quilted stars in the body of the quilt.
The **8** P & A blocks are set square and on-point.
Assembled and hand quilted in Massachusetts.

Hooray for the Red, White, and Blue 54" x 53"

An unusual set of **16** full blocks is coupled with **20** half blocks that form a sawtooth border. This arrangement makes joining blocks of different sizes possible. Assembled and machine quilted in Georgia.

During the Grieving 57½" x 57½"

Friendship Stars set off **16** diverse blocks against a midnight sky. The symbols in each block reflect a positive response to the grieving process. Assembled and continuous-line quilted in Rhode Island.

Friendship Stars 64" x 80"

Guild members joined together to make **48** of the same traditional block, Friendship Star, in varying hues of red, white, and blue. Machine pieced and quilted in Pennsylvania.

In Remembrance 34½" x 34½"

These **9** blocks, made by quilters from across the country and around the world, represent a variety of emotions as well as quiltmaking techniques. The center block unties and opens to reveal an embroidered rose in remembrance of the victims. Assembled and hand quilted in Colorado.

#2380 • $9.95US

#5203 • $3.95US

#4779 • $6.95US

OTHER AQS BOOKS

AQS books are known worldwide for timely topics, clear writing, beautiful color photos, and accurate illustrations and patterns. From documentation to insurance, handy registers can help protect and preserve your quilt investments.

Look for these books nationally or call
1-800-626-5420